PlayTime® Piano

Kids' Songs

2011 Edition

Level 1

5-Finger Melodies

This book belongs to: _____

Arranged by

Nancy and Randall Faber

Production: Jon Ophoff
Design and Illustration: Terpstra Design, San Francisco
Engraving: Dovetree Productions, Inc.

FABER
PIANO ADVENTURES®

3042 Creek Drive
Ann Arbor, Michigan 48108

A NOTE TO TEACHERS

PlayTime® Piano Kids' Songs is a collection of popular songs that brings special joy to children. The simplicity, humor, and charm of the selections will enhance the enjoyment of early piano for students and parents alike. After all, many of these songs have been passed down from generation to generation!

The songs are arranged primarily in stationary hand positions. Where the student moves out of position, a circled finger number will help show the change. These appealing melodies are excellent for reinforcing note names and interval recognition.

PlayTime® Piano Kids' Songs is part of the *PlayTime® Piano* series. "PlayTime" designates Level 1 of the *PreTime® to BigTime® Piano Supplementary Library* arranged by Faber and Faber.

Following are the levels of the supplementary library, which lead from *PreTime®* to *BigTime®*.

PreTime® Piano	(Primer Level)
PlayTime® Piano	(Level 1)
ShowTime® Piano	(Level 2A)
ChordTime® Piano	(Level 2B)
FunTime® Piano	(Level 3A – 3B)
BigTime® Piano	(Level 4)

Each level offers books in a variety of styles, making it possible for the teacher to offer stimulating material for every student. For a complimentary detailed listing, e-mail faber@pianoadventures.com or write us at the mailing address below.

Visit **www.PianoAdventures.com**.

Teacher Duets

Optional teacher duets are a valuable feature of the *PlayTime® Piano* series. Although the arrangements stand complete on their own, the duets provide a fullness of harmony and rhythmic vitality. And, not incidentally, they offer the opportunity for parent and student to play together.

Helpful Hints:

1. The student should know his or her part well before the teacher duet is used. Accurate rhythm is especially imporant.

2. Rehearsal numbers are provided to give the student and teacher starting places.

3. The teacher may wish to count softly a measure aloud before beginning, as this will help the ensemble.

ISBN 978-1-61677-039-6

TABLE OF CONTENTS

Hand Placement

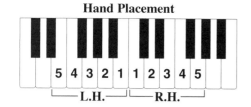

Bob the Builder

Moderately fast

Words and Music by PAUL JOYCE

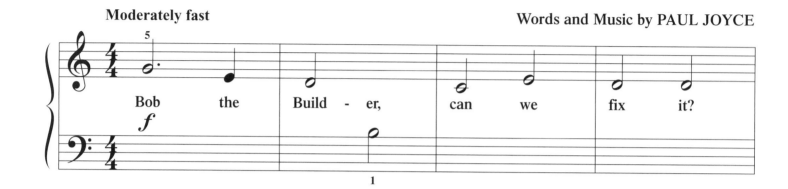

Bob the Build - er, can we fix it?

f

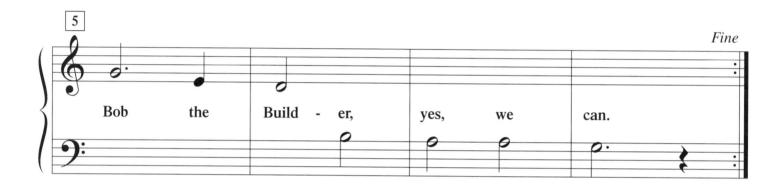

Fine

Bob the Build - er, yes, we can.

Teacher Duet: (Student plays 1 octave higher)

D.C. al Fine (no repeat)

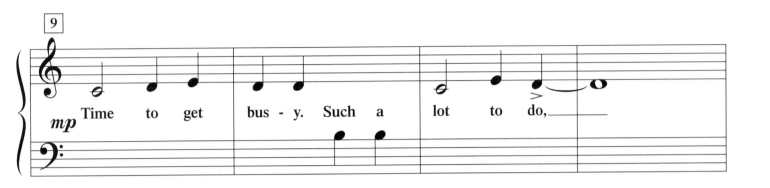

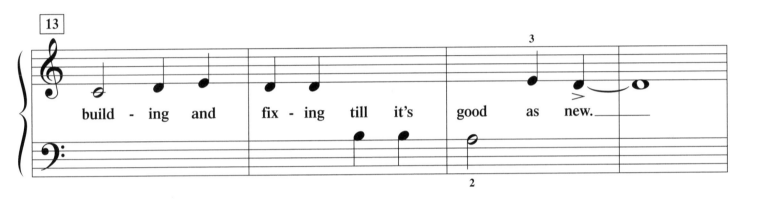

D.C. al Fine
(no repeat)

6

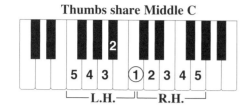

Thumbs share Middle C

Scooby Doo Main Title

Words and Music by
J. BARBERA, H. CURTIN, and W. HANNA

Lively

Scoo - by Doo - by Doo, look - in' for you,
Ev - 'ry - bod - y's here wait - in' for you,

Scoo - by Doo - by Doo, where are you?
could - n't have a show with - out you!

Teacher Duet: (Student plays 1 octave higher)

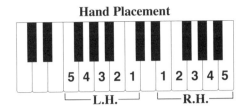

Hand Placement

The Lord is Good to Me

From Walt Disney's *JOHNNY APPLESEED*

Words and Music by
KIM GANNON and WALTER KENT

Happily

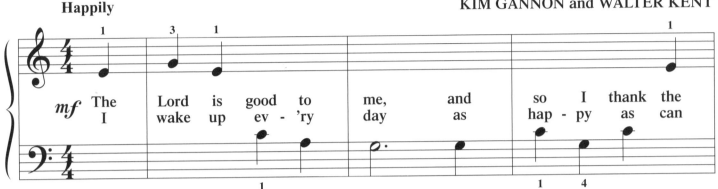

mf The Lord is good to me, and so I thank the
I wake up ev-'ry day and as hap-py as can

Lord, for giv-in' me the things I need, the sun and rain and
be, be- cause I know that with His care my ap-ple trees will

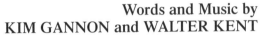

ap-ple tree, the Lord is good to me.
still be there, the Lord is good to me.

(prepare L.H.)

Teacher Duet: (Student plays 1 octave higher)

R.H.

mp L.H.

cresc.   *mf*

FF1039

Let's Go Fly a Kite

From Walt Disney's *Mary Poppins*

Words and Music by
RICHARD M. SHERMAN
and ROBERT B. SHERMAN

Hand Placement

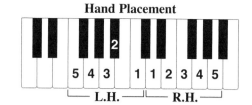

With gusto

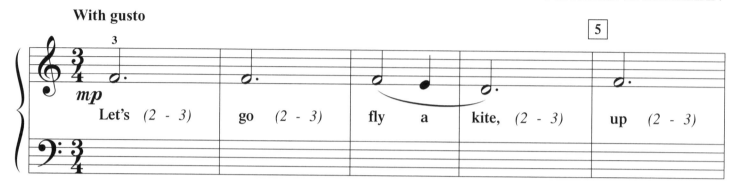

Let's (2 - 3)   go (2 - 3)   fly a kite, (2 - 3)   up (2 - 3)

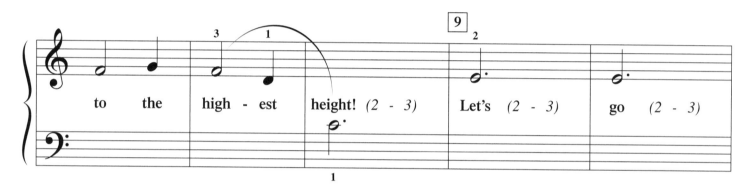

to the high - est height! (2 - 3)   Let's (2 - 3)   go (2 - 3)

Teacher Duet: (Student plays 1 octave higher)

10

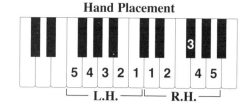
Hand Placement

I Can Be Your Friend

Words and Music by
PHIL VISCHER

Rather fast rock

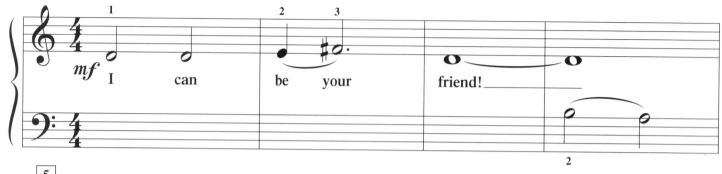

I can be your friend! _____

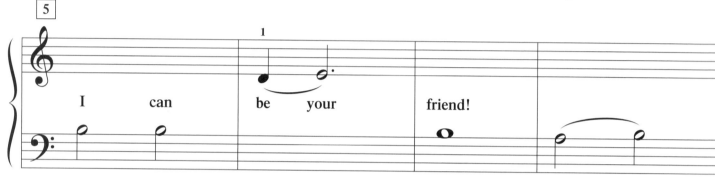

5

I can be your friend!

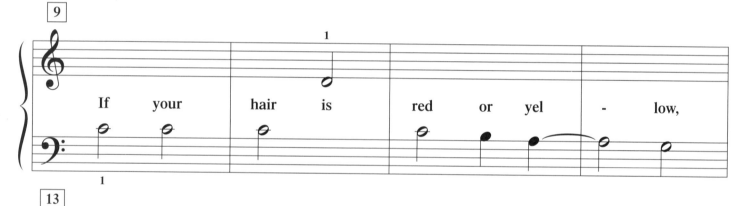

9

If your hair is red or yel - low,

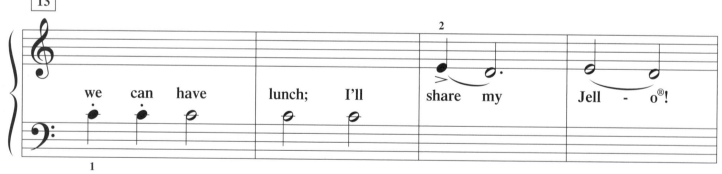

13

we can have lunch; I'll share my Jell - o®!

Teacher Duet: (Student plays 1 octave higher)

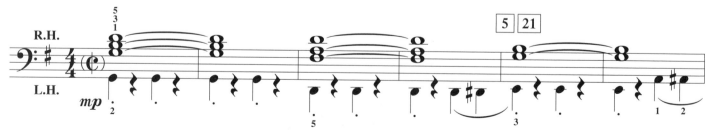

C is for Cookie

Words and Music by
JOE RAPOSO

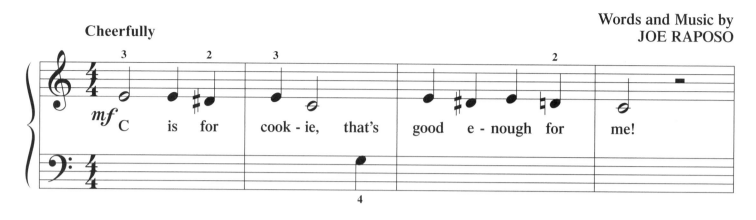

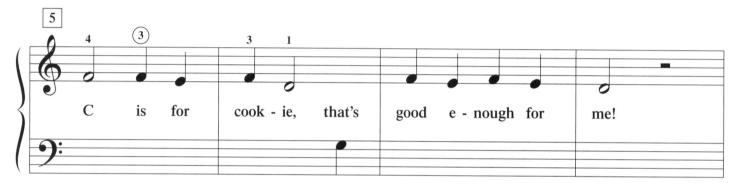

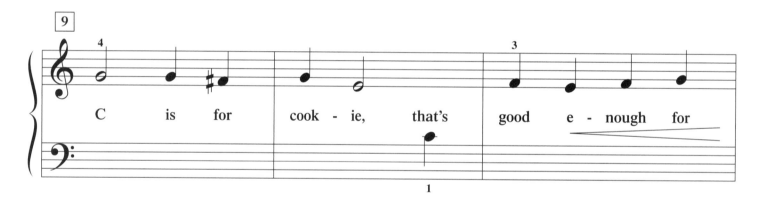

Teacher Duet: (Student plays 1 octave higher)

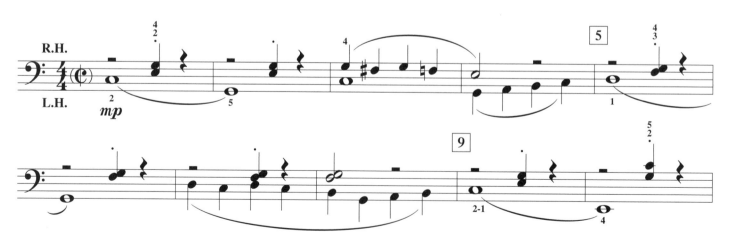

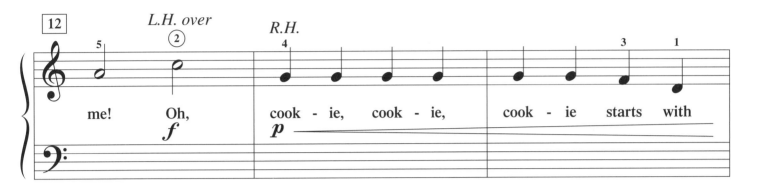

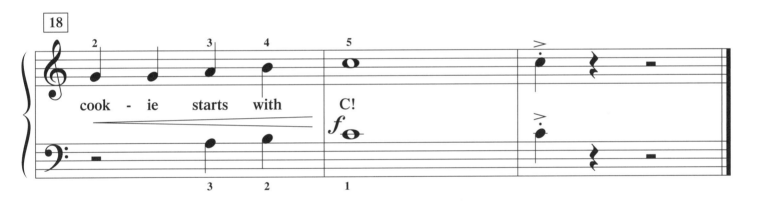

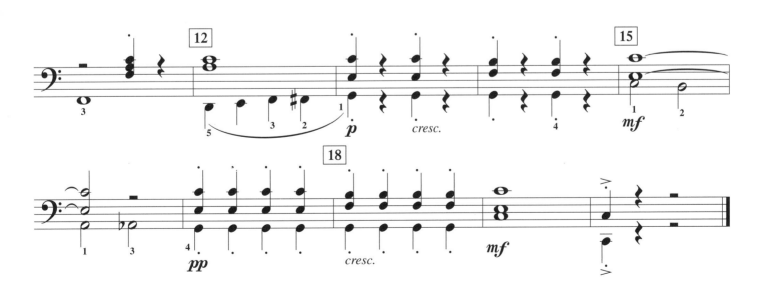

Oh, What a Beautiful Morning

From *Oklahoma!*

Words by OSCAR HAMMERSTEIN II
Music by RICHARD RODGERS

Teacher Duet: (Student plays 1 octave higher)

Ten Chocolate Cookies

Lyric by CRYSTAL BOWMAN
Music by NANCY FABER

Moving along

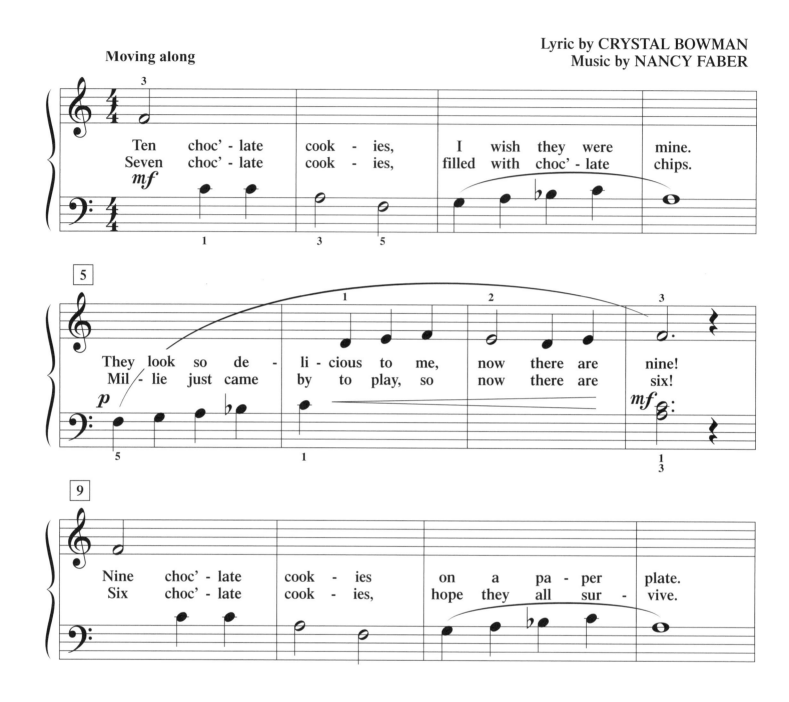

Ten   choc' - late   cook - ies,   I   wish   they   were   mine.
Seven   choc' - late   cook - ies,   filled   with   choc' - late   chips.

They   look   so   de - li - cious   to   me,   now   there   are   nine!
Mil - lie   just   came   by   to   play,   so   now   there   are   six!

Nine   choc' - late   cook - ies   on   a   pa - per   plate.
Six   choc' - late   cook - ies,   hope   they   all   sur - vive.

Teacher Duet: (Student plays 1 octave higher)

Kit - ty jumped up on the coun - ter, now there are eight!
Sis - ter woke up from her nap and now now there are five!

Eight choc' - late cook - ies, wish there were eleven.
Five choc' - late cook - ies, who's at the door?

Broth - er just came home, so now there's seven! Count 'em,
Fa - ther just came home, so now now there's

1.

four, three, two, one... I'll eat the last one, now there's (1 - 2) none!

2.

27 a tempo

1. D.C. (with repeats) 2. 27 a tempo

M-I-S-S-I-S-S-I-P-P-I

Lyric by BERT HANLON and BENNY RYAN
Music by HARRY TIERNEY

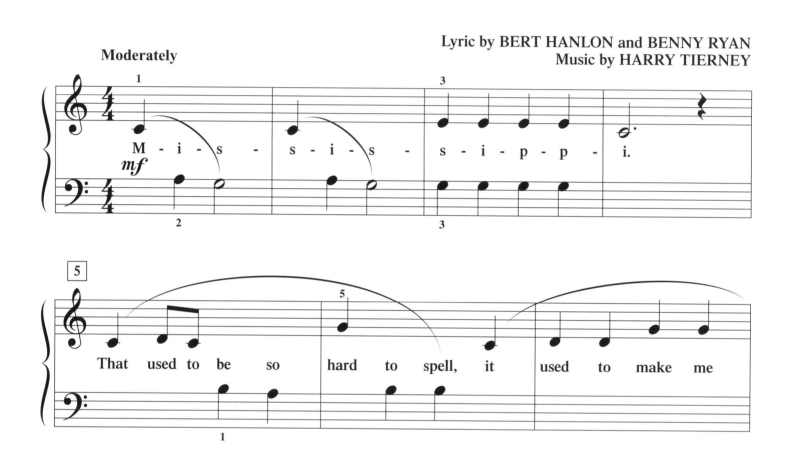

Teacher Duet: (Student plays 1 octave higher)

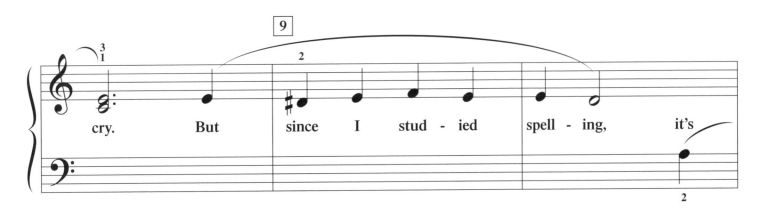

cry. But since I stud - ied spell - ing, it's

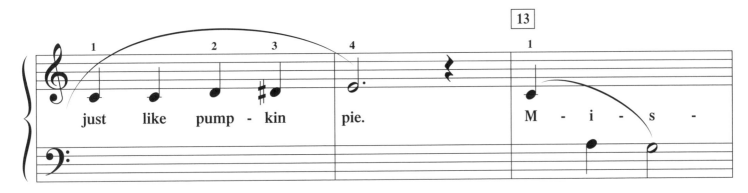

just like pump - kin pie. M - i - s -

(Move R.H. higher)

s - i - s - s - i - p - p - i.

17 *Write letters in the blanks to spell Mississippi!*

p _ _ _ _ _ _ _ _ _ _ _

17

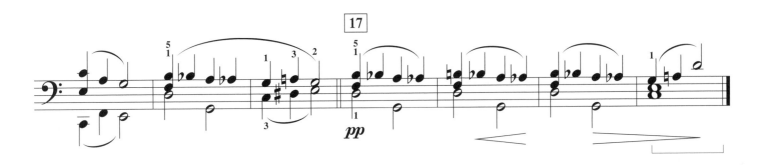

pp

Ferdinand the Bull

From The Walt Disney Production
FERDINAND THE BULL

Lyrics by LARRY MOREY
Music by ALBERT HAY MALOTTE

Teacher Duet: (Student plays 1 octave higher)

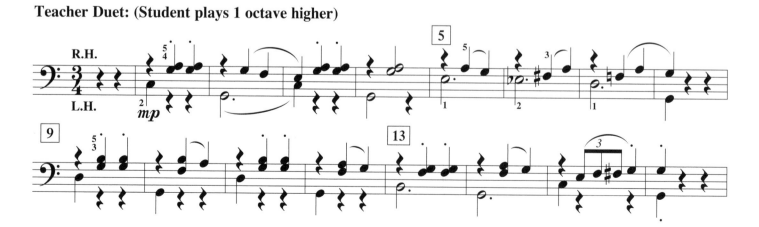

I Swallowed My Gum!

Lyric by CRYSTAL BOWMAN
Music by NANCY FABER

Moderately fast

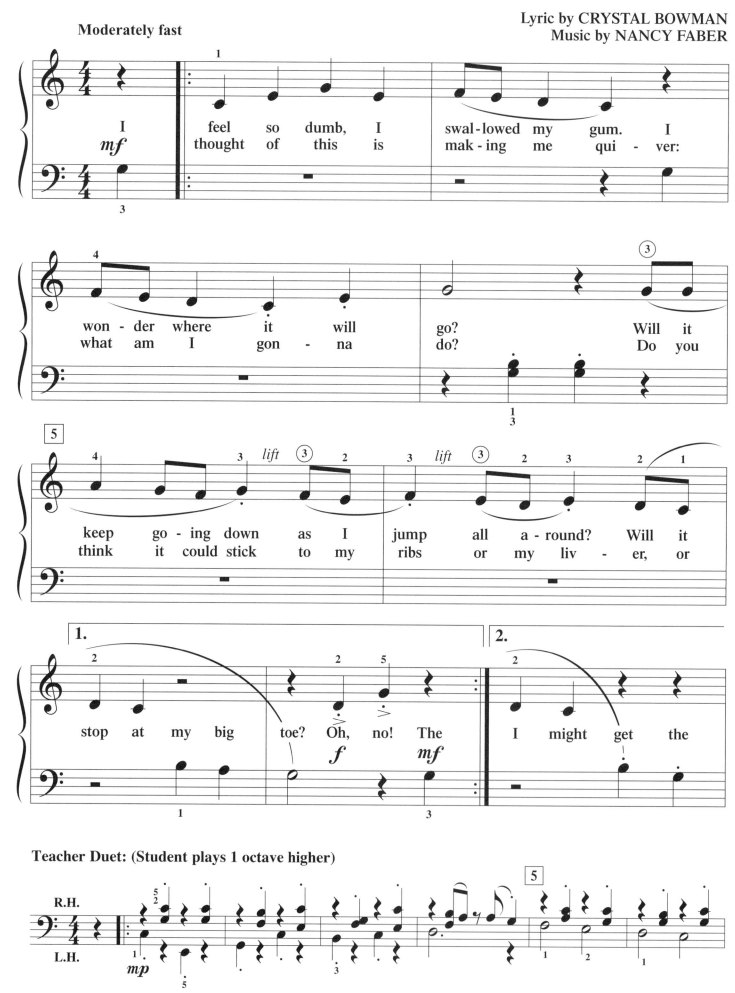

Teacher Duet: (Student plays 1 octave higher)

flu.   Oh!   Should I call the doc - tor?

Go look for my moth - er?   Should I call the po -

lice?   While I   con - tem - plate up -

on ___ my fate, I   think I'll have an - oth - er   piece!

MUSIC DICTIONARY

p	*mp*	*mf*	*f*
piano	*mezzo piano*	*mezzo forte*	*forte*
soft	medium soft	medium loud	loud

crescendo (cresc.)
Play gradually louder.

diminuendo (dim.) or *decrescendo (decresc.)*
Play gradually softer.

SIGN	TERM	DEFINITION
	a tempo	Return to the original tempo (speed).
>	accent	Play this note louder.
D.C. al Fine	*Da Capo al Fine*	Return to the beginning and play until Fine (ending).
⌢	*fermata*	Hold this note longer than usual.
	Fine	End here.
1. ‖ 2.	1st and 2nd endings	Play the 1st ending and take the repeat. Then play the 2nd ending, skipping over the 1st ending.
♭	flat	Lower the note a half step (the nearest key to the left).
▬	half rest	Two beats of silence.
♮	natural	No sharp or flat, just the letter name (a white key).
	pick-up note (upbeat)	An incomplete first measure. A pick-up note(s) leads to the first full measure. Often, the last measure will also be incomplete. Then, the combined value of the first and last measure equals one complete measure.
𝄽	quarter rest	One beat of silence.
‖: :‖	repeat signs	Play the section within the repeat signs again.
rit.	*ritardando (ritard.)*	Gradually slow down.
♯	sharp	Raise the note a half step (the nearest key to the right).
	slur	Connect the notes within a slur.
	staccato	Play *staccato* notes detached, disconnected.
	tie	A curved line connecting the same notes. Hold for the combined value of both notes.
4/4, 3/4, 2/4	time signature	Two numbers at the beginning of a piece (one above the other). The top number indicates the number of beats per measure; the bottom number indicates the note receiving the beat.
▬	whole rest	A whole measure of silence.